MY LOVE AFFAIR WITH A DOG NAMED MOOSE

James D. Bailiff

Published in the United States of America

ISBN 978-1-961507-69-2 (SC)

JDB Publishing
222 West 6th Street
Suite 400, San Pedro, CA, 90731
retrev1@frontier.com

Ordering Information and Rights Permission:

Quantity sales. Special discounts might be available on quantity purchases by corporations, associations, and others. For details, contact the publisher at the address above.

For Book Rights Adaptation and other Rights Permission. Call us at toll-free 1-888-945-8513 or send us an email at admin@stellarliterary.com.

CONTENTS

DEDICATION

To my beloved wife, Beverly, and our children, Cheryl, James, Scott, Richard, Douglas, Michael all of whom loved Moose

INTRODUCTION

My wife, Beverly, and I loved and appreciated animals—animals that belonged to other people. Through the years, many of our friends were pet owners—primarily of dogs and cats—and when we visited in their homes or while walking in our neighborhood, we frequently found ourselves giving attention to their pets, speaking to them, rubbing their fur, and even holding them in our laps.

From time to time, Beverly and I spoke of how nice it would be to have a puppy. But our conversation usually led us to the reality that both of us were heavily involved in our demanding careers, leaving little time for anything else. We reasoned that it would not be fair to have a pet and not have the time to nurture and enjoy it.

I retired in 2002 with Beverly following in 2005. Prior to each, we occasionally spoke of acquiring a pet, but delayed serious discussion until our retirements arrived.

A few months following Beverly's retirement, I asked her, "Now, that we're both retired, would you like to pick up our discussion of acquiring a pet?" Continuing, I asked, "What about a nice little puppy?" Beverly's response was measured, but somewhat positive. "Let's do some homework," she said. "Is it a dog we're looking for? If so, what size, temperament, and appearance are we interested in?"

That's all I needed to spring into action. We both seemed to be interested in a puppy, but the field of possibilities was wide open. Both of us began to research the issue. While we had not settled on the breed of puppy we wanted to acquire we did decide on some criteria. We wanted a puppy that would not grow into a large dog; one that would not shed, was easily trainable, and would be good around children. We also agreed that we wanted a puppy that would be in good health and had a good pedigree. We were cautioned about going to a pet store to purchase because, according to our information, such an option increases the possibility of getting a "faulty" puppy, or one whose pedigree could not be adequately ensured. Once we had decided on the breed, we concluded that our best option was to go to a reputable breeder.

At the time, we were not sensitive enough to be motivated toward animal shelters where, as we now know, there are scores of desirable puppies needing a home. Oh, we knew that option was available, but we were not adequately sensitive to it. Besides, we were looking for purity of breed. For us, that held a stronger promise of getting a healthy animal.

In the first quarter of 2005 after finally deciding to search for a Yorkshire Terrier, Beverly and I contacted a "Yorkie" breeder located in Naples, Florida. We expressed our interest in acquiring a male puppy whose adult weight prospects would be a maximum of five to seven pounds.

From our description, the breeder concluded that we were looking for a male "runt of the litter" and told us she was expecting a new litter within days.

In about a week she called with the good news: "A new litter was born last night and the runt is a male, just the little boy you're looking for." By the end of the week, we drove down to Naples to meet him. She brought him out and presented him to us. Hairless and blind (his eyes were still closed), he moved awkwardly in my cupped hands. I sat down, placed him on my knee and proceeded, gently, to rub his head. He responded by raising his fragile noggin to greet me with little squeaks. Beverly and I fell in love with him on the spot.

We wouldn't be able to take possession until the end of an eight- week period so, filled with excited anticipation, we returned to Sarasota and began marking time.

During that period, the breeder made an appointment to bring the puppy for a visit to our home. At the time of their visit, he was seven weeks old. We were delighted by the progress of his development. He had hair—a beautiful blend of black and reddish blond—dark, piercing eyes, and energy that catapulted him playfully across the floor of our family room. He was so positively responsive to us that we fell in love with him all over again.

Departing with our precious puppy, the breeder invited us to pick him up at her Naples home in one week. She would have his papers all in order.

The week of waiting was filled with conversation reflecting our delight and anticipation. Amidst it all, I asked "What shall we name him?" After we considered several names, Beverly remarked: "He is going to be so small. Let's give him a name that will enhance his self-esteem. Let's name him 'Moose.' Such a name should balance his small size by helping him to feel bigger." "Moose," it was and shall always be!

In our final consultation with the breeder, she talked about diet and training. Her dietary suggestions turned out to be less on target than those regarding his training. Moose's tummy required a special diet, we soon learned. Her directions regarding house training were spot on: "Any time you take him out of his cage (the cage was a special requirement during house training), proceed to the yard and give him an opportunity to relieve himself. When you leave the house for a period of time, always, upon your return, take him out immediately. That way he will soon learn that outside in the grass is the place to do his business. Moreover, when you go away from the house without Moose, keep him in a 'limited' area for the period of your absence. That area became our relatively large utility room in which we placed his comfortable bed and a container of water, along with a baby gate at the door. Moose immediately adapted to that arrangement; so well that when he saw us preparing to leave the house, he would go directly to his little pad and relax.

We became a happy family, the three of us, with Moose at the center of our affection. We had him for thirteen years,

years during which we loved one another deeply, eating, playing, learning, walking, and travelling together. Moose has left an indelible and positive imprint upon us and our extended family.

Following our thirteen years of living with him, we are so delighted for the richness Moose brought into our lives and those of our neighbors and friends. Blest was the day we decided to bring him into our home that soon became his home, too. Now that he is gone we are filled with rich memories that will continue to be a source of inspiration for the remainder of our lives. Later, I will say more about Moose's decline and death. That story, too, is a source of inspiration.

For now, however, I invite you on a journey as I describe several of our routines. Following that, I want to share some significant episodes we experienced together. It is my hope that this journey together will provide windows through which you may be able to visualize and appreciate Moose's character and behavior.

CHAPTER ONE: ROUTINES

Eating our meals, brushing our teeth, attending to chores, etc., are Important routines that help us to get into and through the day with a sense of order. So, too, for our pets--routines help them to develop habits that serve them well.

Early on, we began to introduce Moose to routines. In his really healthy and energetic days, during which he preferred to sleep in our bed, Moose would fall asleep soon but change his sleeping position a few times during the night. As morning broke, he would move closer to me and place a gentle lick upon my face. When he was sure I was awake, he signaled that he wanted to come under the cover where he would press his body against my leg, turn on his back and invite me to rub his belly. After the belly rub, he would launch a series of turns—somewhat like a chunk of meat turning on a rotisserie—until I had massaged him thoroughly, front and back. That done, he was ready to emerge from under the covers, hit the ramp leading to the floor, and let me know it was time to go outside.

In his later days, when Cushing's disease and a collapsing trachea sapped his energy and made breathing a challenge, Moose preferred to be in his sleeping pad placed on the floor at the foot of our bed. At daylight, he would awaken, move to a position near the head of our bed where I lay sleeping and, with gentle and muffled sounds, would usher me out of my sleep. From there, I would greet him verbally as he moved closer, beckoning me to dangle my feet over the edge of the bed and softly rub his arching back with the bottom of my foot.

Typically, I would get out of bed and walk into the nearby master bath, there to begin my morning routines concluding with shaving. Always, he followed me there to position himself in the shower stall, letting me know that he wanted me to pour a glass of water upon the floor for him to lap.

I can see it so clearly in my memory. I turn to see Moose standing in the shower stall, looking at me with those black eyes, wagging his tail, and licking his lips. I would say, "Oh, my boy is ready for a drink!" at which he would bob his head—as if to say "yes."

From there, we would go outside. His trek from the garage was certain as he moved directly across the driveway for his "morning pee," then down the driveway and across the street for his other work. He followed a very specific route for this and so many of his activities.

Returning to the house, we were ready to consume breakfast. By that time, "Mom" had his meal ready, consisting of a plate with eleven little pieces of prescription canned food, along with one and half cooked and cut green beans or a spoonful of cooked green peas. As he vigorously consumed all this, carefully cleaning up any parts which had fallen on the floor, Beverly and I were reminded of a vacuum cleaner sucking up everything in its path. From there he would move to the table where I sat eating, there to sit silently until I reached the melon portion of my meal. He loved watermelon and sparkled when I would fetch a piece for him.

After breakfast, when I had finished taking my vitamins, Moose positioned himself in the family room near my recliner. There he would toss his little rag dog on the floor and look at me in such a way that I knew it was time for me to sit down on the floor and play with him, tossing the toy for him to retrieve. After a period of tossing and fetching, he let me know it was time to move on.

Typically, moving on meant going to my study (office) to read the newspaper and begin my work at the computer. Moose always followed my tracks to that area. Arriving, he would lie down on the floor near where I was working, occasionally raising his head to see what I was doing, perfectly at ease with simply being together.

By mid-morning, Moose would rise from his resting spot, come to my side, look up at me and bark, announcing that it is time for us to go outside to sit in the sunshine. As we exited through the garage he would stop at the door, wait for me to get my beach chair, and we would proceed to a spot where I sat as he wallowed on his back until finally settling to lie in the sun. Sometimes he would signal that he was ready to go back inside, but more often, he would wait until I asked, "Are you ready?" Immediately he would jump up and follow me.

3

Typically, we would return to the study where I would continue working as he lay on the floor relaxing.

Noontime had its interesting routines as well. Always, near noon, he would announce his readiness to eat. With his tail wagging, he salivated as Beverly or I prepared his lunch; then launched into it as it was placed on the floor beside the table at which we ate. Occasionally he would look up at us to confirm that his world was in order; then finish his eating only to approach the main table to explore the possibility of more food from one of us.

Realizing that Beverly and I had finished our lunch, Moose would signal that he was ready to go outside for relief just before accompanying me into our bedroom for his "greenie" treat and a nap.

As he consumed his treat, I proceeded to brush my teeth. When I had finished, Moose had usually positioned himself in the shower stall—just as he had earlier in the morning—thereby announcing that he was ready for me to pour that glass of water for his consumption.

That done, he would run to the side of the bed where he waited for me to pick him up, place him upon the bed and proceed to join him by lying down beside him for a nap. Once I was positioned, he would move his body next to mine, settle in, and signal sudden sleep with his light snoring.

The early to mid-afternoons were filled with a combination of playing with Moose and working on my yard or in the study. If it was yard activity, I would tell

Moose, "I'm going out to mow the yard" at which announcement he would position himself near the front door where he could see me through the window as I worked outside. If the option was working in my study, he would accompany me there and lie on the floor near my desk.

Late afternoons/early evenings became our walking time. Attaching his leash, I would lead him down the street and onto the golf course. Usually, we walked along the shores of the lakes that border every fairway at the Serenoa Golf Club, there to retrieve lost golf balls. Often, Moose seemed as interested as I in finding them. When spotting one under a bush, he would often stop and signal me, not unlike a pointer who spots his hunter's prey.

While finding golf balls was important to Moose and me, most of our time was spent walking, often for two miles or more. Occasionally, when the fairway was wide and long, and the danger of alligators in the water was a minimal threat, I would detach his leash, and let him go. Typically, he would go 25 or 30 yards, stop and look back at me, signaling that he wanted me to put some distance between us. When I had gone 50 to 100 yards—while he sauntered around smelling the ground—I would turn and call for him. At that point, he would begin a furious run to reach me, resembling, with his billowing hair, small body, and short, churning legs, a tumble weed rolling relentlessly toward me. At the end of the run, he would jump into my arms panting, licking my face, and assuring me that this was one of the best days of his life.

Other day-time routines grew out of our trips to the bank, store, or park. Often he would accompany me to the bank's customer service drive through. The staff knew us well and, as soon as our banking transaction was done, our helper would typically send Moose a nice doggie treat. To ensure that the treat would not be forgotten, Moose would position himself prominently on the seat where the cashier could see him clearly. As soon as the treat arrived, he wanted to attack it but, familiar with the mess of crumbs he would leave on the car seat, I would often hold onto it until we arrived back at the house. My efforts to conceal the treat were somewhat effective but, knowing that the treat had arrived and was somewhere in the car, he would begin a diligent search for it. When we had arrived back at the house and parked in the garage, still searching, Moose exited the car, all the while looking at me with eager anticipation. Soon the treat was revealed and consumed!

Other trips took us to Home Depot where his adventure became riding in the shopping cart. Usually very large and noisy, the carts initially threatened him but as I folded down the plastic seating area and placed there a comfortable lamb-like piece of fleecing which Beverly had acquired for this purpose, he learned to settle down and enjoy the ride. Inside the store, he seemed to delight in several things—the nice cool air-conditioning, the experience of rolling up and down the various aisles, examining the store's offerings, and the frequent encounter with other dogs in their owners' carts. Of all components of the shopping experience, he seemed to enjoy most our encounter with the folk who stopped to visit with him, speaking to him in soft, gentle tones, and reaching out to rub his silky hair. Always, he responded in a friendly fashion as if to say, "It's good to see you too!"

At times, our afternoon adventures included a visit to a park where there were other dogs. Whether large or small, Moose perked up in their presence. His greeting to them was always gentle and non-threatening which elicited from them a similar response. If a large dog came toward him quickly to check him out, Moose would register his dissatisfaction, simply by turning away, expressing a lack of interest. If any dog growled at him, his usual style was simply to ignore them and go on his way. But what he seemed to enjoy most about the adventure was the freedom to run in the open spaces. Typically, unless there were strict leash rules, I would unleash him and off he would go, actively exploring the surroundings. Almost always, when I called him, he would respond promptly. With the passing of time, I was increasingly impressed with how well Moose responded to my verbal commands.

Late evening and night time were filled with interesting routines, too. Throughout the evening Moose would rest on the floor, rising occasionally to get a drink of water or to ask for a treat. When bedtime came, Beverly and I would follow our routines of taking our medications and supplements, while he watched us from the spot where he lay on the floor, following our every move with those dark eyes. In the process, I would reach for his toothbrush. This seemed always to heighten his interest. Moving toward him

I would say, "Time to brush teeth!" As I approached and reached for him, he would stand so I could put my hands around his belly and carry him to a chair where I could sit, lay him on his back in my lap, and proceed with teeth brushing.

"Open!" I would say, at which command, reluctantly, he would open for access to his teeth, letting me know that this was not his favorite--nor even a desired—experience. He seemed to recognize its necessity, however, and usually cooperated with the process.

Immediately following the brushing, I would leash him to take him for his last outside visit of the day. He would march to his favorite spot, lift his leg, and relieve himself, after which I would always tell him, "Good boy, Moose, good boy!"

As bedtime came, I would direct him to get onto our bed. Up the ramp he would scamper and onto the bed where he proceeded his ritual scratching and searching for a spot on which to lie, there to wait for Beverly and me to come to bed, tell him "Good night," and kiss him on the forehead.

As I reflect upon Moose and routines we established together, I am convinced that for him, those routines, provided security. They became established "habits" that were not only familiar, but also predictable. He knew what was coming at significant points in the day. In my imagination, he was able to anticipate the good and pleasant, such as scampering upon the wide fairways of the golf course. At the same time, I imagine him bracing for those experiences—such as teeth brushing—all while sensing that he would emerge from the ordeal with his mouth feeling fresher and his sense of taste improved.

My unofficial and inexpert counsel to any dog owner is to establish routines within which your pet can operate with a sense of SECURITY, anticipation, and happiness. The familiarity of daily routines makes their day sparkle.

CHAPER TWO:
EPISODES
Moose and Water

Moose was very young, and he had been in our home a short time when, one day, I was relaxing in our pool, drifting on an air mattress. He had followed me onto the pool deck and was lingering in the shade as I began to float. I had just closed my eyes when I heard it, the sound of a plopping splash. Initially, I continued to relax when, suddenly, it occurred to me that the sound may have been caused by Moose hitting the water. Indeed, when I looked, there he was paddling for dear life in an effort to reach my float. Immediately, I rolled off the float and gathered him into the safety of my arms. With his short legs and the depth of the water, he could never have found footing. He seemed so excited to be rescued and began a vigorous licking my face in appreciation. After spending some time reassuring him, I took him to the edge of the pool and released him. His reaction was to shake the water from his body and hasten to the shade of the pool deck, there to take a position behind a chair. When I beckoned him to return, he was totally noncompliant, as if to tell me he was finished with the pool.

This experience seemed to traumatize Moose and make him defensive around water for the remainder of his long life. For example, when Beverly began to run water for his bath, he would make himself as inconspicuous and unavailable as possible. After he got into the bathwater he would shiver and shake and look pleadingly toward me to rescue him. Eventually he became more adapted to baths, learning that they were quite harmless and that they would be followed by the warm breeze of a hair dryer and his release to a pleasant treat.

Reflecting upon the pool experience, I have frequently given thanks that I was aroused from my relaxation on the air mattress to discover Moose paddling frantically in the water. I am convinced that, for the rest of his life, he carried a pronounced anxiety about being around water. Subsequently, I was very careful to protect him from potential anxiety producing situations either by total avoidance or by gradually introducing him to new things to minimize their threat level.

Each summer we spend some time at a vacation site on Sugar Mountain in Banner Elk, North Carolina. Moose loved the mountain air and, particularly, our walks in the beautiful park the municipality has created. A walking trail runs the length of the park through a valley between Beech Mountain on the north and Sugar Mountain on the south. Down the valley, alongside the walking trail, flows a beautiful mountain creek with its crystal clear and refreshingly cool waters.

The first couple of years of our taking Moose to the site, we led him near the creek. Upon hearing the running water, he resisted moving closer. We did not force the issue but moved on up the trail, allowing him to relax. In the third summer, as we neared the creek, I picked him up and walked slowly toward the stream, speaking to him in soft tones. Arriving at the shore of the stream, I let him listen as I tossed a couple of stones into the water; then moved on. The following summer, as we approached the stream, hearing the sounds, he led me to the stream, stood beside it for a moment, then, putting his front paws into the water; he lapped it with his tongue. After a momentary pause, he walked out into the stream's shallow pool, manifesting no anxiety. From then on, Moose seemed always eager to engage with the stream and its cool refreshment, apparently free of anxiety.

Although he maintained his caution around our pool back home, Moose did allow me to carry him into the pool on occasion. At other times, when he approached the edge of the pool and peered cautiously over into the water, it seemed as though his anxiety about the water was decreased but that his memory of his initial experience continued to curb his enthusiasm for swimming.

From this episode regarding the pool, I learned not to force Moose in any given situation. I learned the importance of letting him explore possibilities and allow him to decide his level of engagement.

Moose and Other Animals

On our frequent afternoon/evening walks Moose was introduced to snakes, gators, cranes, deer, squirrels, hawks and other species. He seemed interested in all cases, but it was his nature—perhaps because of his small size—to be cautious and defensive. For example, one afternoon, as we walked on the golf course, a long thin black snake came out of the bushes and began slithering its way across our path. Immediately, Moose took notice and very cautiously moved toward the snake, observing it from a safe distance. At one point the snake stopped and moved into a semi coiled posture, turning its head toward Moose. Moose stopped and, standing at a distance, observed the snake with keen interest. After a while, I led Moose away. It was not long until he had developed interest in other "neighbors."

Sand Hill cranes are numerous in Southwest Florida and, particularly, in Serenoa, a suburban community of Sarasota where we live. Upon seeing these interesting birds, Moose took great delight in dashing at them, causing them to run or fly away. It seemed to give him a sense of power. On occasion, a crane might exhibit a defensive posture by spreading its wings to give it a larger, more threatening appearance, but this seemed not to phase Moose who ran relentlessly toward the cranes until they flew or ran away. At such times, I kept a cautious grip on his leash for fear that the cranes may retaliate by attempting to impale Moose with their long, needle-sharp beaks. Thankfully, that never happened.

Until he recognized the futility of chasing squirrels, Moose ran toward them, hoping to catch one. I remember on one occasion when, to his astonishment, he did "catch" one. We were walking on the street when, in an adjacent lot, he spotted a squirrel sitting on its haunches and chewing on an acorn. He pulled at the leash. When I cut him loose, he launched toward the squirrel with all the speed he could muster. By now he was accustomed to the squirrel immediately darting away from his onrush, but this particular squirrel, apparently preoccupied with his meal, did not sense Moose's approach, resulting in a collision that knocked the squirrel aside and staggered Moose. Alarmed, the squirrel ran up the nearest tree while Moose shook himself and peered quizzically at the shivering squirrel, then at me, as if to exclaim, "What in the heck just happened?!"

Moose always seemed defensively sensitive to his surroundings. For example, as we walked one afternoon, a large bird's shadow came upon us which caused him to duck his head and move toward me for protection. Another day a large osprey flew down close to Moose and me. Moose reacted in his usual defensive way. Thankfully, the osprey simply swooped down, decided we were too formidable a challenge for him, and chose to locate himself in a nearby tree from which he seemed to observe us.

I've seen hawks and other large birds swoop down to catch a rabbit and carry it off for consumption. Aware that Moose was about the size of a rabbit, I was always on the lookout for them. The possibility of his being carried away by a bird led me never to let him be alone outside.

Moose on the Loose

On a rainy day, our doorbell rang. There stood my neighbor, Paul Cherry who, in his outstretched hands, was holding Moose covered with mud, dripping wet. As soon as I opened the door, Paul exclaimed, "The Moose is loose! I found him running furiously up the street after a large dog, growling and barking threateningly, with cars whizzing by. I was concerned that he might be eaten by the big dog or hit by a car. So, here he is, all in one piece!"

I was flabbergasted! Thanking Paul profusely and getting Moose cleaned and dried, I sat down to reflect on how this could have happened, concluding that when I had gone into the garage earlier, Moose followed me. Being unaware of his presence in the garage, I left him there, re-entered the house, and returned to my office work. Apparently, the open garage doors had become a tantalizing invitation for Moose to begin his adventure.

I held him in my arms and talked to him about the danger of the situation and how good it was to have him back safe and sound. He listened and, when I had finished, he gave me his characteristic affectionate lick, letting me know everything was Okay.

To this day, I continue to be somewhat mystified by this adventure. It was not like Moose to go out on his own. He had not chased big dogs before, and always seemed aware of the danger of traffic. I've concluded that, confused and frustrated about being left alone in the garage, he had proceeded to the behavior Paul had described. So, following the incident with a prayer of thanksgiving that it had all turned out well, I let it go.

Beverly and I enjoy a large and loving family who, in Moose's earlier days, loved to gather at our house on special occasions. On one such occasion, we had fifteen people milling around in the large area that constitutes our kitchen and family room. The crowd was loud as the grandkids were running around chasing one another and Moose. These precious "grans" were the age at which they enjoyed grabbing him and pulling his ears. I had noticed such activity going on and sensed that Moose was not comfortable with the situation.

At one point, as the chaos grew more intense, I leaned against the kitchen counter, talking with one of our sons. I felt a familiar fur ball touching the backside of my legs. It was Moose who had run there to find shelter. I picked him up and held him in my arms where he settled in the protection of dad's embrace.

I suspect that Moose's small stature amplified the threat of such experiences. He must have felt extremely vulnerable among the "forest" of legs and pounding of feet. While I was never happy to see Moose anxious, I did find his rush toward my protection to be pleasant. This experience of his strong trust in me just strengthened the bond between us.

Under normal circumstances, when someone came for a visit, there were usually fewer people and less chaos. At such times we sat on the couches in the family room involved in soft conversation. Typically, in such situations,

Moose came to me or to Beverly asking us to place him in our laps where he relaxed, apparently happy to have visitors and listening to every word.

Reporting this episode, I realize afresh how important it is to be "tuned into" our animals, reading their levels of comfort or anxiety, in order to provide just what they need from us. Such an atmosphere binds us together with our pets in a way that creates an amazing sense of love and fulfillment.

Moose as Partner in Ministry

I derived considerable pleasure when Moose participated in my work as a pastor or chaplain. I remember beginning an interim ministry with the Central Christian Church (Disciples of Christ) in Orlando, Florida. At the close of the Sunday morning worship service, I chose to introduce my family. Earlier, during the singing of a hymn near the beginning of the service, Beverly had slipped into the sanctuary with Moose. A few people noticed this lovely lady with a dog and, as was later revealed, wondered about their identity and presence.

At the end of the service, before the benediction, I asked for a point of personal privilege for the introduction of my family. Beverly and I had pre-arranged for her to take a position at the entrance to the sanctuary near the center aisle. At my signal, she would release Moose. To get this done, I needed to introduce Moose before introducing her. I hammed it up a bit, indicating that my first introduction may seem a bit unusual; then declared, and "Now meet our only son still at home! This is Moose Bailiff!" Immediately Beverly released him and he came running down the aisle full speed, jumping into my arms and licking my face. The congregation roared. When they had settled, with Moose still in my arms, I introduced Beverly as my wife and Moose's mom. She walked down the aisle and there we stood to the applause of a delighted congregation.

I don't know how much members of that congregation remember about my sixteen months with them. But I do know that many present that day recalled and commented upon how "precious" it was to have Moose and Beverly introduced that first Sunday of our interim work.

I was delighted by an e-mail I received from one of the church members upon learning of Moose's recent death. She wrote: "I'll never forget how very precious it was when Moose ran down the aisle to your arms on our first Sunday at our church."

Subsequently, I would begin a five-year ministry as Chaplain of the Bay Village Retirement Center in Sarasota. In addition to general pastoral care for the residents and staff, the bulk of my work as chaplain was to conduct Vesper worship, Bible Study, Singing and fellowship time with residents of our nursing center and our assisted living center.

On numerous occasions Moose, attended by Beverly, would participate in our Vesper worship service. He was received well and adored by the participants. But where he seemed most appreciated was among those residents of our nursing center with whom I met for half an hour each week to sing, play games, and tell stories. The policies allowed and supported the presence of "care dogs" in that setting. Realizing the importance of bringing a loving animal to interact with the residents, I invited Beverly to bring Moose on occasion. That first visit was hugely successful. I introduced him to the group and he walked to every participant and seemed very pleased as each reached to feel his silky hair and encounter his affection. Between Moose's visits, residents would ask me to bring him back again. It became a mutual affection arrangement. They loved Moose and Moose loved them.

Now retired from chaplaincy there, along with Beverly, I recently attended a luncheon at Bay Village to honor volunteers. As we were greeted by friends, many asked, "Where's Moose?!" As we shared news of his recent demise, we could see the hurt on their faces and were showered with their memories of appreciation for him and with their loving support of our own grief at his loss.

Moose on Sugar Mountain

Each summer Beverly, Moose and I spend several weeks in the Southern Appalachian Mountains near Boone, North Carolina. If you are driving in from Atlanta, Charlotte, Richmond, or any other major regional city, Boone feels like a leap into another world. On leaving Boone, to ascend the mountain on Highway 105, one comes to the smaller towns of Linville and Banner Elk. If Boone feels like another world, Banner Elk may feel like another galaxy. It is a fine expression of village life U.S.A.

Moreover, its distinctive Appalachian culture seems vastly different from that with which many of us in more urban and mainstream America may be more familiar. It is not unusual to see folk plowing a field with a horse drawn plow or old sages sitting on a country store porch swapping stories. Often one can hear energetic conversations about some aspect of religion. On the local radio station Sunday morning programming presents abundant offerings of Gospel singing and style of vigorous preaching that is stimulating and challenging. Village folk interacting with one another while relaxed on their porches or lawns or in a restaurant reminds the onlooker that there are people resisting the devilish rush of life by taking time to engage one another. There is a distinctive accent, sprinkled with folksy sayings, along with lots of "aints," "up yonders" and the like. Billed NASCAR caps, tobacco-stained beards and bibbed overalls are popular.

It's not unusual to see on display old whiskey making "stills" and big brass apple butter making containers.

It is not my intention to sound condescending. Rather, I want to emphasize distinctions in a culture that has resisted the homogenization process which permeates so much of what we urbanites experience. Some of these folk who may look and sound like old country bumpkins are very astute. Among them are chemists, physicians, musicians, professors, pastors, farmers, blue collar workers, and the like.

I have found that so many of us outsiders, in the process of experiencing that culture, find much about it that is beautiful. I sense that many of us make a considerable effort to identify with it and to treasure it, rather than to attempt changing it. It seems that this beautiful sub-culture is more genuine and creative than much of the monotonous sameness in which our wider culture has immersed us.

And there is so much natural beauty expressed in the mountain ranges that ascend into the clouds and fold into lovely valleys. Streams and rivers are everywhere, most of which are clear to crystal clear, relatively uncontaminated with the pollution to which many of us are constantly exposed.

Experiencing the culture, one senses that great numbers of us join the native folk in an effort to protect ourselves from that which Richard Louv, in his book, *The Nature Principle,* calls a "nature deficit syndrome," that condition into which one drifts when she or he has gotten away from engaging with the natural environment. Thus, it is not unusual to hear folk talking about trees, birds, dogs, cows, clouds, mountains, thunder, lightning. They tend to describe how their experience of these seems to put them in touch with something deeper, even sacred, resulting in an increased sense of finding one's meaning and purpose. So, one can hear an old Oscar Keener talking about how he and his "hoss" (horse), over the years, have become like brothers, or an Anne Trivette, describing the meadow behind her house, along with its rabbits and raccoons, as a gushing source of inspiration.

All that and more, is Banner Elk to which Beverly, Moose and I have returned time and time again. No wonder, when we are away for a while, our hearts yearn to drink from its fountains of inspiration afresh!

From our first summer there with Moose, we sensed that he was as enamored by the mountains and the culture as we. He reflected awareness of the difference in the flat lands of Florida and the mountains surrounding Banner Elk. For example, as we entered the condo, perched on the side of Sugar Mountain at an altitude of 5,200 feet, through the wide glass, we were immediately confronted with a panoramic view of the southern Appalachian Blue Ridge Mountain chain. It looked and felt like we were on top of the world. Moose took notice that something was spectacularly different as, very cautiously, he stepped through the sliding glass doors onto the porch, whose wooden floor featured large spaces between boards through which one could see the seemingly distant ground below.

Moose's fascination reminded me of an incident that occurred years earlier when we took our first grandchild, Jimmy Lee, to the mountains. Arriving after midnight, he had fallen asleep. I carried him inside and put him to bed. When he awoke the next morning, stirred by the bright sun rays piercing the windows, he looked out and, for the first time, saw the surrounding mountains. His reaction was so precious: "Grandpa, look how tall the trees are!" Living in Florida, where trees have virtual uniformity of height, and possessing no concept of mountains, he did not understand the topography of "high ground" and "low ground." To his young mind, the trees of Carolina had grown very tall!

To my mind, Moose was having a similar, somewhat ambivalent experience! Connecting the responses of my beloved Yorkie and my precious grandson was exhilarating for me.

As time unfolded, I introduced Moose to the experience of hill and mountain climbing. For example, the very next day, we climbed the road leading to the base of Sugar Mountain's summit. At the end of that road is the edge of forest land with its meandering trail leading to the summit. I thought of how Moose might react to this narrow trail, bordered by bushes and small trees and was delighted when, on his leash, he fell right into step behind me, stopping often to smell the bushes and to mark his territory. He seemed comfortable and secure in the experience. In less than a mile, we broke out of the wooded area directly onto the summit of Sugar. Before us was the spectacular view of Elk valley in which the town of Banner Elk is located, bordered on the north by the sweeping slopes of Beech Mountain whose pinnacle pierced the sky like a giant finger, on the east by Grandfather Mountain, named for its profile of an old man's face as he lies in rest. To the west, like a silent sentinel, Hump Mountain, registered its presence alongside the Sugar, the Beech, and the Grandfather, all joined in an alliance designed to protect and to inspire.

From there, Moose and I carefully climbed onto a rock cliff that protrudes from Sugar's top. The climb required me to lift Moose to the ascending shelves of the rock and resting him there while I climbed to meet him. We did this repetitively, until we had reached the very top. I felt this process may make him anxious but there was no sign of anxiety. Rather, he seemed to be as curious and eager as I to get to the very top. Soon we arrived and the view was even more spectacular than the one before. We sat down on a rock shelf, Moose on my lap, and both of us scanning the panorama before us, our turning heads, perhaps, favoring a submarine's searching periscope.

Moose seemed as "into" the experience as I. Having spent my childhood and adolescence in the area, I examined the geography meticulously, identifying spots on the mountains where I had been foxhunting with my father or climbing with my peers. I found myself listening for conversations that had long passed, and to the long past barking of old Sam and Drive, dad's registered Walker hounds, as they chased a red fox through the valleys and on the mountains. The inspiration of the view and the resurrection of those memories triggered old gospel songs I had learned as a child, including "Precious Memories," so popular then and now.

While all this was going on inside me, I had to wonder what was going on inside my Yorkie. As I looked into his beautiful black eyes, rubbed the silky hair of his body, and, in my embrace felt his breathing, I imagined that he was experiencing his own inspiration and making his own memories. Occasionally he would look up at me and, lifting his head toward me, to place an affectionate lick upon my face as if to say, "Dad, this is a wonderful experience. Thanks for letting me share it with you."

Moose loved the cool air and breezes of the mountains. I sensed that he was also impressed with the variety of flowers, landscaped so beautifully around our condo. He reflected an affinity for the rabbits and squirrels that often appeared when we were hiking. The bumblebees seemed to be a huge mystery for him. The friendly faces of the Sugar Mountain and Banner Elk communities, along with their tender treatment of our precious canine son seemed to endear Moose to them and strengthen his bond with us who had introduced him to such environs.

When we return to the mountain this summer, Moose's absence will leave a silent ache in our hearts balanced with the sweet memories of our adventures there.

CHAPTER THREE:
MOOSE'S PHYSICAL DECLINE

It happened one evening following our routine of brushing Moose's teeth. When I had finished and placed him on the floor, he began to experience difficulty with breathing, gasping for breath while unable to inhale sufficiently. Alarmed at his distress, we called our vet, Dr. Evelyn Andre Hansen, who lives in our neighborhood, just a few blocks away.

Dr. Hansen knew Moose well from having treated him for most of his life. During that time, she had done two surgical procedures to remove stones from his bladder, had nursed him through bouts with allergies, and prescribed a balanced diet that would prevent him from irritating his always sensitive stomach. During that time Moose had bonded with her, and she had embraced that bond.

"Dr. Hansen," Bev exclaimed into the phone, "Moose seems to be having a serious problem with his breathing, both Jim and I are afraid this may be a life-threatening event!" "I'll be right over," she said. In just moments the doorbell rang. Moose was so affected by the breathing episode that he didn't follow his usual routine of running to the door with eager anticipation of welcoming a visitor.

For a moment, she observed Moose; then picked him up, speaking to him in soft tones while stroking his body gently. In a few moments he settled into a normal breathing routine.

She asked us to describe what had happened just prior to this event. I related how we had just gone through the teeth brushing routine with Moose who, as usual, lying on his back to give me easy access to his teeth. Dr. Hansen concluded that a combination of his discomfort with that position triggered an episode in "reverse breathing" which was dramatic enough to be alarming both to Moose and to us. Her counsel: "Just lighten up on teeth brushing and let's see if that brings an end to this reverse breathing thing."

Subsequently, I changed the procedure, brushing his teeth less frequently and, those times when I did brush, attempting to do it without rolling him onto his back. To compensate for reducing the regularity of brushing his teeth, we purchased cleaning gel to use each day for the purpose of reducing tartar build up and to make his breath fresh. This seemed to work satisfactorily.

Though they were rare, other episodes of this reverse breathing would come, less severe but concerning to us. In each case, Moose seemed to shake it off.

In time, however, he seemed to have some difficulty with breathing while doing fairly moderate activity that he had formerly done without signs of distress. For example, when we walked a considerable distance, he would begin breathing heavily. This was new to us. We had a history of walking for two miles without any signs of stress on his part. Formerly, he and I would walk around the perimeter of our Serenoa community during which time he showed no signs of distress and would return to the house wanting to engage in floor play.

Regularly, he would do his running tumbleweed thing which I described earlier, at the end of which he seemed to have ample energy reserves.

Now, Moose was growing less able to be vigorous without an onset of heavy breathing and apparent tiredness. Discussing this with his vet, we agreed with her suggestion that she perform some tests, one of which was to do some x-rays. That process revealed that his trachea had collapsed and was minimizing his breathing efficiency. When he was not exercising vigorously, he seemed fine, but the moment he exerted himself physically, he manifested symptoms of serious breathing distress.

Surgery was an option, but Dr. Hansen recommended against it, feeling that Moose was not a good candidate for a successful outcome. Beverly and I agreed and we opted for medication management.

For about a year, Moose seemed to get along quite well. While he could not sustain the vigorous protocol of the past—tumbleweed running, taking two-mile walks, etc.—he remained active by taking shorter, more relaxed walks, playing in the floor, etc. His interest in people, in other animals, happy living, food and being close to family was maintained at a high level for a period of about two years.

In his twelfth year, it was obvious to us and to his vet that Moose's health's decline was accelerating. Walking a few blocks seemed to exhaust him. He began to have less interest in floor play; particularly chasing after toys and returning to me. It was sad to see him indicate an interest in that exercise but, when begun, to fade very early and walk away. He began to sleep more, seeking out various places on the floor where he could lie flat, either on the carpet or tile where, it seemed, he could breathe better. Though, years earlier, we had acquired a ramp up which he would scamper to take his place beside us in bed at night, he reached a point where his energy level seemed not to allow that nightly ascent. Soon, thereafter, we began lifting him onto the bed. Initially, with that process, he would settle into a spot, staying there the remainder of the night to awaken fresh the next morning. In time, however, when we awoke in the morning, we would find him on the floor, having moved there during the night. We concluded that this change signaled that he was more comfortable, particularly with his breathing, on the hard surface of the floor.

Already Moose was breathing very heavily when we had walked less than a block. We would stop and let him rest. Soon we realized his walking days were behind him. Because of his love of being outside and the adventure of moving through the neighborhood to greet all his human and canine friends, Beverly and I knew we had to improvise.

One day, Beverly told me that she had been researching pet appliances and had found a stroller designed for small dogs. We agreed that this was just what we needed to sustain Moose's love of roving through the neighborhood.

The stroller arrived, and what a marvelous vehicle it was! Its four wheels gave it remarkable balance and maneuverability. Its space for Moose was sized just right with windows for him to see both when he was lying down and when he was sitting.

Initially, we wondered how he would respond to it. When we introduced it him, he seemed to be a little concerned about being put into the containment area, but he complied without much resistance. As we began to move, he seemed to relax, perhaps because he had grown familiar to riding in shopping carts. So, here we went, down the street, dad, mom, and Moose in his new stroller. We could see him adjusting to the viewing portals, crouching down to see where we were going; even lying down, on occasion, to test the lowest viewing window. We found his adjustment period to the stroller to reflect typical Moose behavior. For example, when riding in the car—on our trips to the bank or to Home Depot, Moose always fixed his attention on the route. At all times, he seemed to feel it important to know exactly where he was going. I did not read this as mistrust in us, but as a Yorkie characteristic of always wanting to have a measure of control.

It was not long before Moose had taken to the stroller like a duck to water. Soon it was clear that his favorite riding position was to sit uprightly in the stroller. This position raised his head to a point above the vehicle's sides where he had a full view of the territory. As an added bonus, it provided him eye level contact with the Golden Retrievers among whom were some of his favorite friends. He could greet them without having to look up or cowing below them as they affectionately pressed their giant bodies upon him.

Though Moose was in clear decline, he was still the sociable, lovable, puppy we had always known. I feel certain that he was aware of his growing limitations, particularly his progressive difficulty of breathing. By now, even under circumstances of normal relaxation, he was breathing heavily and for the most part not from his chest area, but from his abdomen. His difficulty was distressing to us. We could read his discomfort and, through the communication skills which had developed between Moose and us, we could see him looking at us as though to ask, "Mom and Dad, what is happening to me?" In spite of this, however, he did not appear to become grumpy, irritable, or depressed. For him, life was still fulfilling and love flowed both from and to him.

Simultaneous to his decline in respiration— particularly in the latter stages—Moose reflected other symptoms of decline, particularly with respect to his vision. For example, one day, following our mid-morning time in the yard, as we were coming back into the house, I had opened the door so he could enter. He paused, looked in the general direction of the door, then proceeded to walk into an adjacent wall. He backed up and successfully renegotiated his entry. While in earlier days he entered with a flying leap over the high step leading from the garage into the house, I noticed, now, that he was much more cautious and less energetic.

A couple of weeks before Moose's death, we made an appointment for him to see Dr. Hansen. His breathing had become more labored and, to my mind, he was manifesting symptoms of congestive heart failure. I was concerned that his lungs may be collecting fluid, making his breathing difficult. Listening to my description, Dr. Hansen agreed that Moose appeared to be experiencing some congestive heart failure. She gave him a diuretic and asked us to watch the results. A few days following, Moose seemed to be more relaxed in his breathing, but continued his lethargy and his lengthy periods of sleeping. His appetite, however, remained strong. He loved meal time and those delicious concoctions Beverly made for him. Moose never ceased coming to the table, following the consumption of his own food, to explore the possibility of a morsel or two of people food.

On Sunday, April 22, just a week prior to Moose's thirteenth birthday, we returned from attending worship at our church. As we entered the house, I did my usual call: "Where is my boy, Moose?!" As I rounded the corner which allowed me to peer over the baby gate and into the utility room where Moose stayed when we were away, there he was, standing and wagging his tail, ready for us. I removed the baby gate and led him outside to relieve himself. When he finished, I noticed a new sound to his coughing. Somehow, it seemed more intense and the wheezing a bit more pronounced. But he shook it off and we came back into the house where Beverly had prepared his lunch plate.

After consuming his meal, Moose seemed a bit pensive and cautious. In a few moments, he had begun to breathe heavily. That soon grew more intense and he went into what I call "distressed" breathing, breathing rapidly, but apparently not getting sufficient air.

I picked him up, placed him beside my ley legs on the flat part of the recliner with full expectation that he would recover. That recovery never came. In just a few moments, he leaned into my right thigh with considerable pressure; then I could see his little body totally relax—like an accelerated version of a cut flower wilting in the hot sun. Suddenly, it dawned upon me that Moose had died. I took his very limp body in my arms and began to massage his chest with a faint hope that the procedure may revive him. Oddly the lifelessness of his body, like a living thing leaped out to me, confronting me with the fact that this precious canine son who had been our delightful companion for thirteen years was gone.

Beverly and I were stunned. Both of us were weeping. Finally, I said to her, I think Moose's heart, enlarged over the years, just gave out. Both of us were struck by how abruptly this had happened. We sat in reflective silence for a while. I continued to hold Moose in my arms and, along with Beverly, released my emotions.

After a few moments, out of our felt need to have her pronounce our little guy's death as a fact and to let her know that one, whom she loved, had passed, we called Dr. Hansen. In a few moments, she and her husband were at the door. Their sensitivity to our distress was like a drink of cool water on a very hot day, just what we needed. After attending to us, she went to Moose's bed, upon which I had laid his body, picked him up and wrapped him in a blanket.

Beverly and I had already decided we wanted to have our beloved canine son cremated. Dr. Hansen concurred and facilitated that process. "I'll take him home with me and keep him tonight, if that's all right with you. Come Monday, I get the process moving forward," she said softly

I didn't know what that process would look like, but, as promised, in about a week, we were able to pick up Moose's cremains and bring them home. His ashes were placed in an ornately carved wooden container. There was also a plaster disc with his paw print. Also, there was a little book which focused upon how to deal with our grieving process. Both of us are deeply grateful for the work of Belspur Oaks Pet Crematory in Sarasota, for the tasteful and meaningful managing of the cremation process.

The response of our veterinarian staff, family, friends at large and neighborhood has been a Godsend. Dr. and Mr. Hansen were there for us in those tender moments immediately following Moose's death. The lovely card we received from her staff, bearing the signatures of all those who had worked with Moose, was most meaningful. Our children and grandchildren, scattered throughout the United States have been there for us, sharing memories and offering sympathy. Our neighbors have said and done things that have supported us considerably with gifts of food, phone calls, and hugs. Members of churches in which we have participated have responded with the sharing of warm memories they have of our beloved Moose.

It has now been about three months since his death. While it still stings when we speak of him, the sting is growing less intense as it gives way to pleasant memories. As I sit typing, with a slight move of my head, I can peer around my computer screen to see one of my favorite pictures of Moose, alongside which are the paw-printed disc and the container of his ashes. I frequently look at the scene. When I do, I'm impressed with how Moose appears in the photograph, looking directly at me with his head slightly tilted, his ears sticking straight up in the air, his silky, multicolored hair shimmering, and those little dark eyes saying, more loudly than ever, "Dad, thanks for all the precious times we spent together. I miss and love you." (And, as I write this, I have to dry my tears, tears of pain, thanksgiving, love, memory and hope).

I'm about ready to proceed to the last chapter, but I must not go there before sharing with you something for which Beverly and I are most thankful. Because of his rapid decline, we had begun to prepare ourselves for what would have been a huge decision, namely, to have Moose euthanized. Both of us loved him too much to let him fall into a tortuous journey into the valley of acute suffering and progressive vegetation. Therefore, we had determined that, when the time came, in consultation with Dr. Hansen, we would make that decision. But we both knew that such a move would be extremely painful for us. As it happened, we did not have to make it. It was made for us and not before we had been able to walk with our beloved through the green pastures, beside the still waters, and into the valley of death. It was as though we had wrapped Moose in our love and shared with him not only the exciting verve of life, but also the mystery of death, right up to the appropriate time for him to leave us on that mournful Sunday when he died, pressing his little body into mine as if to say a final and loving goodbye.

Now, I'm ready to move to the delicate, but extremely meaningful, last chapter. Please go there with me.

CHAPTER FOUR:
WHAT NOW?

Just like that, a new situation confronts Beverly and me. There was that first evening, and morning, and month without Moose. The house seemed so empty. Sometimes, our hearts felt emptier. I turn the corner, expecting to see him, or sit working in my study expecting that signal that tells me he wants to go outside for our morning exposure to the sun. I awake each morning imagining him sitting beside the bed with that distinctive whimper designed to see if I am ready to rise so we can begin our day together.

Beverly and I frequently speak of Moose. She talks about how she still plans her day's activity in order to meet Moose's need. When arriving back at the house following a brief jaunt into the community I find myself calling out, "Moose, we're home. Where's my boy!" When I go to bed at night, I walk by the spot where he spent his nights on the floor and where, every night, I would get down on the floor beside him and kiss him goodnight. At that spot I pause, for it has become "holy ground."

Beverly and I check with one another regularly to see how we are progressing through our grief; how we are adjusting to Moose's absence. Though the move is slow, it is sure. Moreover, it is movement with meaning. The pain we feel is a reminder of our love for our little canine guy. I have found myself saying about his death, "It hurts for sure, but I wouldn't have it any other way." Any absence of pain would indicate that the quality of our relationship with Moose was not as precious as we had thought. The pain, while very uncomfortable at times, reveals to us new and fresh dimensions of our love for him. It reminds us that there is purpose in any suffering we may experience if we let ourselves become engaged with it and open ourselves to the fresh nuances of meaning which, because of its sensitive nature, it can bring to us.

Increasingly, Beverly and I find that we are blessed with scores of memory pictures. Regularly we find ourselves remarking, "Remember when…." Those moments remind us that we carry Moose in our hearts in such a way that he will never be forgotten. Our daughter, Cheryl, gave us a precious throw cushion on which is a picture of me holding Moose. At the top of the picture are these words: "No Longer by Your Side, but Forever in Your hearts!" Indeed, our memories form a life-giving spring whose waters will always slake our thirst.

Though we are stung—sometimes stunned—by Moose's absence, increasingly we are aware of his presence. We can still feel the silky quality of his three colored coat of red, blond and black. I still feel the texture of his tongue as it moves against my leg, not only to express deep affection but also to give him a taste of dad. Frequently, I feel the warmth of his body snuggling into mine as I sit in the recliner or lie in bed. Moose is everywhere and I'm trying to "tune in" so I can pick up his every "vibration."

Beverly and I were walking one recent evening. Our path intersected a golf cart crossing where Moose and I so often began our late evening hikes onto the golf course for some of the adventures described earlier. Our walk together was coming to an end, when I remarked, "Honey, I think I'll leave you here and trek up the course for a while." "Fine, but be sure to get on in before dark," she replied.

I struck out by myself, walking the cart path past the tee box of the fourth hole. The fairway opens wide, bordered on the right by a beautiful lake and on the left by the cart path beyond which lies another expanse of the divided fairway. Immediately, I imagined unclipping Moose's leash to let him run upon the wide expanse, calling him back to me as he neared the lake. I could see him acknowledging the call, turning his body and "tumble weeding" his way back to my side.

As I turned the corner, around the fourth green, I passed the spot where, in an experience about two years ago, Moose and I had an unforgettable encounter. That evening our walk followed one of our typical summer rains. As we turned this same corner, my eyes—always on the lookout for what lay ahead of us—spotted something lying on the cart path about 100 yards ahead. Instantly I thought, *snake*! As we got closer, I could see clearly a large water moccasin stretched upon the cart path. Apparently, it was moving out of a nearby swampy area on its way to a lake that lay across the west of the cart path. While it was lying still, it seemed very alert to our approach. That it was not coiled indicated to me that it was not preparing to strike. I observed it for a while, noting the white mouth from which another name for this species is derived—*COTTONMOUTH*. The creature was not very long, perhaps 3 to 4 feet, but very muscular, reminding me an image of a weightlifter's arm coming to mind.

After observing the snake for a few moments, during which time I was holding tightly to Moose's leash, we began to move around it, giving it a wide birth. When we had moved on up the cart path, I looked back and the snake was gone, apparently turning back into the protection of marshy bushes from which it had earlier emerged.

I remember how Moose had no reaction to this encounter. I have suspected that, given his (by that time) declining vision, and the snake's lack of motion, it had more the appearance of a large piece of wood rather than that of a live creature. As a result, it is likely that Moose never saw it. For me, however, this was a genuine memory maker, memory rooted not only in my fear of snakes but of the potential for an encounter that could have turned out badly.

During this evening of walking upon territory that I had shared so often with Moose, I experienced many memories. As I walked on the fairway leading to the seventh green—another large expanse on which Moose loved to frolic, I walked close to the lake that borders the south side of the area. It's a beautiful body of water, featuring lots of beach area. Paying particular attention to that, I remembered the evening Moose and I, following the same path, had seen a very big alligator lying in the setting sun. His head was extremely large from which the length of his body protruded, giving him the appearance of a large battle tank. Immediately, I recalled how, on the evening of this encounter, I gripped Moose's leash more tightly and walked briskly across the fairway, heading north to get ourselves out of a potential harm's way.

As I continued my solo walk, I was reminded, at every turn, of my precious little walking companion. When I left the course, turning down Taeda Drive toward home, I suddenly realized that I had just exited one of those precious zones in which my departed Yorkie and I had mysteriously been reunited in a way that filled me with joy. Arriving at home, I shared the experience with Beverly who responded, "That's why I did not offer to accompany you. I felt you were reliving the many times you and Moose had walked the course."

As I reflect upon our 13 years with Moose, his death, and, now, the aftermath, I feel that to have had our time together was a special gift; that if there is nothing else, our lives have been wondrously affected by our time with him.

But I keep hearing these questions down deep in my being: Is there something more? May there be another experience with our precious Yorkie that is more than a memory, more than his living on *in our hearts*? As I have contemplated that question I have come to realize that it's one so many of us ask about ourselves: Is there a life beyond our death? Will we encounter, again, those we have loved and lost?

I do not open this section of my writing lightly. My spirit tells me that such questions introduce us to very delicate and sacred territory. If we dare go there, we must recognize that we are about to contemplate things that transcend the usual and ordinary. Then, too, I have paused to consider whether, by considering an afterlife that involves Moose, I am simply fantasizing. But, as I consider that possibility, my faith remembers the biblical vision of *ultimate destiny* which transcends the rational limitations of this earthly life. This experience calls me back from the edge of the limitation precipice, reminding me that the hope I am feeling is rooted in something much deeper than psychological projection or fanciful thinking.

Therefore, these questions—Is there life beyond our death? Will we encounter, again, those we have loved and lost?—evoke from me a humble "yes." I emphasize humble because of the *mystery* of the concept of life after death. My humility does not imply doubt. Rather it is designed to provide an avoidance of both the arrogance and naiveté of some who seem to "have it all figured out" and are confident that they can describe that profound level of faith's promise as clearly as they can describe their last vacation to the beach.

In other words, I am secure in affirming the promise, but stand in reverence and in awe of its content which is contained in the New Testament concept of "Heaven." To my mind, Heaven is a symbol for the richness of that ultimate reality. It affirms that our loving and faithful God is fulfilling the promise to lead creation to the destiny for which it has been and is being created. To my mind, while the fullness of that is beyond that which our time-and-space-conditioned finitude can comprehend; we can depend upon its veracity.

When talking of things like creation of our world (the beginning) or its consummation (the end), we have entered an arena much of whose nature remains a mystery. For example, consider the following observation of theologian Hans Kung in his notable book *On Being Christian:*

> The Bible starts with creation and sees the end as the consummation of God's work on his creation. Neither the "first things" nor the "last things," neither the dawn of time nor the end of time, are directly *accessible to experience.* There are no human witnesses. World creation and world consummation can be described only in *images:* poetic images and narratives for what is fundamentally ineffable. (p. 219)

Ineffability does not mean unreality. Rather, it points to that which lies beyond the boundaries of logical explanation; that which must be accessed through poetic images. To such belongs the issue of Heaven.

I am suggesting, therefore, that we need to speak of heaven with some caution because that ultimate reality is something about whose nature we know only in part, not wholly or fully. That ultimate destiny, though we may have a taste of it in our experience of that which Jesus calls the *abundant life,* transcends our earthly experience and remains a profound and life-giving mystery filling the faithful with a vibrant hope.

For example, when the apostle, Paul writes of it in his second Corinthian letter, contained in the New Testament, he shares how he experienced either in a vision or in his body, a "tour" of heaven. However, rather than to deliver an arrogant report on that experience, he eases into a description with caution: "... *I heard things which cannot be put into words, things that human lips may not speak"* (2 Corinthians 12: 4). I sense in St. Paul's comment a conviction that, because heaven's quality and beauty are so far beyond our earthly limitations, we are not equipped to comprehend it fully. However, we can live in anticipation of being delivered into that ultimate destiny provided out of our Creator's love for us, believing it to be far superior to anything we can now know or understand in full measure given the limitations of finitude.

By now you may be asking, what has this to do with my story about Moose?! The last few paragraphs represent my attempt to lay the groundwork for sharing my conviction that Moose is involved with that destiny. In an attempt to be open and honest, and to avoid being simplistic, shallow, or trite, I want to share that conviction with *integrity.* Moreover, I want to honor the mystery that St. Paul is honoring in the Corinthian passage. As he, I want to bow in reverence before the mystery; yet bow with fervent hope based on my trust in the love God has for all creation.

You may be thinking, "Okay., I believe in Heaven and I get that it something whose ultimate quality is beyond our finite ability fully to comprehend. But where do you get the idea that animals share that destiny, along with people?"

A general overview of the biblical faith pushes me toward the concept that God's sovereign love and compassion are focused upon rescuing *all* creation from its broken state. Consider, for example, the intentional focus upon the acts of creation in the two *beginning* stories in the first book of the Bible, *Genesis*. There, each act of creation is considered to be both intentional and precious.

Now, fast forward to the last book, *Revelation* which speaks so eloquently of a "new" earth and heaven:

"Then I saw a new heaven and a new earth (which I take to represent the whole sphere of earth [its systems and species] to which heaven will fully come.) The first heaven and the first earth disappeared, and the sea vanished. And I saw the Holy City, the new Jerusalem coming out of heaven from God, prepared and ready....I heard a loud voice speaking from the throne: 'Now God's home is with people. He will live with them, and they shall be his people. God himself will be with them, and he will be their God. He will wipe away all tears from their eyes. There will be no more death, no more grief or crying or pain. The old things have disappeared....I did not see a temple in the city, because its temple is the lord God Almighty and the Lamb. The city has no need of the sun or the moon to shine on it because the glory of God shines on it, and the Lamb is the lamp" (Revelation 21:1-4, 22-23).

Please note how the focus is upon the entire created system (earth for this first century writer); not exclusively upon either individual humans or a collection of us.

In short, I am suggesting that a general overview of the Judeo-Christian faith underscores the concept from our present perspective, has lost its way.

The clincher for me, however, comes earlier in the New Testament, in a very specific passage from St. Paul's letter to the *Romans* in which he focuses upon *all creation* , not just the children of God, groaning to be set free for the heavenly destiny:

*"I consider that what we suffer at this present time cannot be compared at all with the glory that is going to be revealed to us. All of creation waits with eager longing for God to reveal his children. For creation was condemned to lose its purpose....**Yet there was the hope that creation itself would one day be set free from its slavery to decay and would share the glorious freedom of the children of God.** For we know that up to the present time all of creation groans with pain, like the pain of childbirth. But it is not just creation alone which groans; we who have the Spirit as the first of God's gifts also groan within ourselves as we wait for God to make us his children and set our whole being free"* (Romans 8:18-23).

Clearly, let me here affirm my sense and belief that there is a heavenly destiny for *all* God's creation. It involves you and me, all God's people, but it also involves all other species, including animals; which includes my beloved Moose.

Such a conclusion about an *inclusive* destiny feels at peace in my being. It avoids what I perceive to be a weakness in the view held by some that an *eternal destiny* is designed exclusively for human beings.

While I do not impose this wider interpretation upon my readers, I am suggesting that it is consistent with the teaching of the Christian faith and, therefore, worthy of your consideration.

My point in this discussion is to share with you my belief that our precious Moose is within the focus of God's redeeming love; that he shares the destiny that Beverly and I do. So, we settle down to wait for our transport into that beautifully mysterious destiny.

In his death our little guy was so caringly handled by his vet, Dr. Hansen, who wrapped his body in a blanket and arranged for its cremation. Beverly and I treasure the beautifully carved wooden box that contains his ashes, and his paw print so clearly marked on the plaster disc. It is our desire to have a portion of his ashes mixed with ours at our death. These, of course, are sentiment symbols designed to underscore our deep appreciation and love for Moose and our belief that he shares in an inclusive destiny God has designed for all creation.

A related issue to this thinking is the reunion this destiny brings to all who participate in it. Given the transcendent nature of this destiny, we can only *imagine* what that reunion will look like. It is a special environment beyond time and space experience with which we are not, at this point in our journey, directly acquainted. I repeat, reverently, that a description of it from our time and space perspective remains, at best, inadequate.

Perhaps a simpler way to put it is to declare my belief that when I get to heaven, not only will I see our Maker, our Savior, beloved parents, grandparents, children and grandchildren, friends and neighbors, ancient and modern heroes, and new persons I have not previously met, but there, in a state of creation's complete restoration, will also be creation's variety of species. Therefore, my imagination holds that among all those greeting one another in this divine reunion will be a little Yorkie by the name of Moose--recreated in perfection—recognizing Beverly and me and, running, full speed, to leap wildly into our arms, wagging his tail and licking our faces as if to say,

"Oh how wonderful it is to be together again!" At that point I will know that my love affair with a dog named Moose as not ended but, by God's grace, has entered into eternity.

CONCLUSION

Thank you for taking the time to read about my relationship with Moose. I imagine that among you are those who have loved and lost a beloved pet, an experience that introduced you to significant grief. If that has not been your experience, I hope this story has impressed upon you the beauty of the relationship possible between ourselves and our beloved pets.

Tradition has it that St. Francis of Assisi was so close to nature that when walking through a garden he experienced birds ceasing their flight to land upon his shoulder, there to communicate with him in ways that transcended mere language. On one occasion, when a squirrel had come from the forest onto the trail upon which Francis walked, he stopped and addressed his friend with a warm. "Good morning, brother squirrel!"

While not all of us possess Francis' sensitivity to nature, it seems that most humans have a soft spot in our hearts for various kinds of animals. If that is true, I feel that many of you have identified with my relationship with Moose.

With his loyal devotion to me, Moose gave me many gifts. Perhaps one of the most notable of those was the gift of sharpening my sensitivity to the natural affinity we humans have for those precious living creatures with which God has surrounded us. Such awareness means that we are never really alone as long as we can hear the song of birds, the howling of a coyote, the squall of a squirrel, or the chirping of crickets.

Thank you, beloved Moose, for ushering me into a world surrounded with the wonder and majesty of creation. I am so blessed to have experienced you as a distinct incarnation of love and affection. For now, you may no longer be by my side, but you are forever in my heart.

EPILOGUE

In the wake of Moose's death, Beverly and I have talked about acquiring another dog. During our dialogue we have become aware that we are not sufficiently equipped, emotionally, to make that decision now. For example, I am at the point in my grieving at which to consider acquiring another dog feels like a betrayal to our precious Moose. I am aware of how foolish that feeling is, but I am also aware that the very irrational nature of that emotion signals that I have work to do before I am ready for another. When we are out for dinner or some other activity, Beverly continues to feel the need to rush back home so Moose is not left alone too long. In her head she knows better. Moose is not at our house anymore. But the emotional unsteadiness of her heart is a signal that she, too, is in the middle of her grieving process.

The temptation is there. We pick up on puppy photos, puppies on T.V. commercials, puppies in our neighborhood, and puppies riding by in carts at the stores. Recently, I told her of a Yorkie picture I had seen that kindled a fire within to go right out and get that puppy. Thankfully, we are able to read these compulsive temptations as symptoms of our grieving and know better than to yield to them while involved so delicately in that process. Consequently, we have agreed that we will not make a decision on whether to get another puppy until mid-summer by which time we will have returned from summer vacation and will have had another couple of months to continue the grieving process.

At the appropriate time, will we decide to acquire another dog? Will we search for another Yorkie or will we expand our options? We feel quite comfortable with our old and established criteria: a small dog, one that does not shed, is easily trainable and behaves itself around children, etc. The issue for us is: shall we, again, take the plunge that demands so much in terms of time and care investment.

There are other considerations. We need to address the issue of where to go in the acquisition process. Whereas, in the past, we leaned heavily toward acquiring a healthy pet with clear pedigree from a registered breeder, I sense that we are now more conscious of the need to explore the option of searching for our next pet in a rescue shelter. We've learned that there are scores of desirable animals waiting for a good home.

Another issue that figures into our decision is that of our longevity. I am in my 80th decade and Bevely is late into her 70th. How long are we going to be around to care for a new pet? What would happen if a puppy outlasts us? To my mind, these questions do not block our move in the direction of acquiring a new dog, but they do open the possibility of our choosing, not a new born, but one that is older.

You can see, then, that by mid-summer we have some decisions to make. Both of us feel we'll be ready by that time to think and act more objectively. I also sense that we will go looking for another dog that can receive our love and give its own. Yet, for now, Beverly and I both feel that the right thing is to delay our decision to that mid-summer target.

Finally, allow me to tell you that writing these pages as a memoir to our beloved Moose has been one of the most therapeutic things I could have done. Walking back through those thirteen precious years has brought a mixture of emotions from tears to smiles and laughter, all of which were in great need of being released from our hearts.

If you are in the wake of grieving for a lost pet, or about to be, I encourage you to give strong consideration to writing about your experience with your pet. Not only does it aid in facilitating your grief process, but it provides you a written set of memories you can share with your friends and family. The written record will always be there, handy for picking up and reviewing.

Thank you for sharing this journey with us. Hopefully, you have been able to find some blessing in the process. Let us all move forward in thanksgiving for the inspiration our pets bring to us and the hope that their lives, too, were and are fulfilled.

END....

www.ingramcontent.com/pod-product-compliance
Lightning Source LLC
Chambersburg PA
CBHW031236120626
46545CB00003B/1139

9 7 8 1 9 6 1 5 0 7 6 9 2